THE GODDESS ARCHETYPE OF A MYSTIC

Copyright © Nichole Muir, Goddess Wisdom Transformation

Website: www.GoddessWisdomTransformation.com

All rights reserved. No part of this book may be reproduced, stored, or transmitted in any form or by any means—mechanical, photographic, electronic, recording, or otherwise—nor may it be included in any information storage and retrieval system, transmitted, or otherwise copied for public or private use, beyond the "fair use" provisions (such as brief quotations in articles and reviews), without the prior written permission of the publisher.

The information contained within this document is provided for educational and entertainment purposes only. While every effort has been made to present accurate, up-to-date, reliable, and complete information, no warranties of any kind, either express or implied, are made. Readers acknowledge that the author is not providing legal, financial, medical, or professional advice. The content of this book has been compiled from various sources. Before attempting any techniques described in this book, please consult with a licensed professional.

Contents

Chapter 1: The Calling of the Mystic 4

Chapter 2: The Veil Thins 9

Chapter 3: The Ancient Scrolls 14

Chapter 4: The Dream Oracle.................................... 19

Chapter 5: The Ritual of Silence 24

Chapter 6: The Sacred Grove 28

Chapter 7: The Mystic's Challenge........................... 33

Chapter 8: The Alchemical Marriage 38

Chapter 9: The Chalice of Visions............................ 43

Chapter 10: The Hermit's Path.................................. 47

Chapter 11: The Portal of Stars................................. 52

Chapter 12: The Healing Waters 56

Chapter 13: The Shadow Dance 60

Chapter 14: The Circle of Elders 65

Chapter 15: The Phoenix Fire.................................... 70

Chapter 16: The Labyrinth Walk................................ 74

Chapter 17: The Feast of Echoes 78

Chapter 18: The Mirror of Caladriel.......................... 83

Chapter 19: The Oracle's Prophecy.......................... 88

Chapter 20: The Ascension 92

Chapter 1: The Calling of the Mystic

In the quiet village nestled at the edge of the ancient Whispering Woods, there lived a young woman named Elara, whose life was as unremarkable as it was predetermined. Each day, from dawn until dusk, she helped her family tend to their small farm, her hands more accustomed to soil than to the mysteries of the world beyond their land. Yet, despite the simplicity of her life, Elara often felt a strange, inexplicable pull—a call that resonated deep within her, drawing her towards the shadowy trees that bordered her home.

As the sun dipped below the horizon one crisp autumn evening, Elara sat by the window, gazing at the play of shadows amidst the trunks of the ancient trees. Her family had long avoided the woods, heeding old tales of spirits and magic that dwelled within. But to Elara, these stories whispered secrets and promises, not warnings.

"Elara, come away from there," her mother's voice broke through her reverie. "The night is no time for daydreaming."

"Yes, Mother," Elara replied, but her voice lacked conviction. That night, as her family settled into the depths of sleep, Elara's restlessness grew. The call was louder than ever, an almost palpable melody that seemed to vibrate through the very air. She knew that tonight was the night. Slipping from her bed, she dressed quietly and tiptoed out of the house, driven by a force she neither understood nor could resist.

The air was cool and crisp, filled with the rustle of leaves and the distant call of nocturnal creatures. The moon, a slender crescent, provided just enough light to guide her path as she approached the threshold of the woods. The trees stood like ancient sentinels, their branches swaying gently in the wind, beckoning her closer.

With each step, Flara felt her heart beat faster, her skin tingling with a mix of fear and exhilaration. She paused at the edge of the forest, taking a deep breath. The woods were alive with an energy that seemed to hum in tune with her own pulse. It was as if the very earth under her feet was aware of her presence, welcoming her.

"Why am I here?" she whispered into the darkness.

The wind seemed to sigh in response, and as Elara stepped into the woods, the canopy above parted slightly, allowing a beam of moonlight to illuminate the path forward. The woods felt different now, not threatening but enveloping her in an embrace as old as time.

Elara walked deeper into the forest, her eyes adjusting to the dim light. The trees seemed to move around her, their trunks bending subtly as if clearing a path. After what felt like hours, she reached a clearing she had never known existed. In the center stood an ancient stone, moss-covered and inscribed with symbols that shimmered under the moon's touch.

Drawn to the stone, Elara reached out and traced the cool, weathered symbols with her fingertips. A warmth spread through her body, a lightness she had never felt before. The air around her thickened, and the forest held its breath. Then, as suddenly as it had begun, the sensation faded, and the night resumed its chorus.

Confused but exhilarated, Elara knew something profound had happened. She felt connected to the world in a way she couldn't explain, as if the stone had spoken to her in a language beyond words, a language of spirit and of the earth.

As dawn approached, Elara reluctantly left the clearing, the stone, and the silent watchers of the woods. She returned home just as the first light crept over the horizon, slipping back into her bed to catch a few fleeting moments of rest before the day began anew.

The days that followed were filled with mundane tasks, but Elara's mind was elsewhere. She was haunted by the memory of that night, the feelings of connection and awakening that had surged through her. She knew she could not ignore the call of the mystic path that had been revealed to her.

Driven by a newfound purpose, Elara began to seek out old books and scrolls in the village, pouring over texts that spoke of the ancient mystics who had walked similar paths. She learned of their ways, their rituals, and their deep communion with the natural world. Each page turned added fuel to the fire that had been lit within her that night in the forest.

As she delved deeper into her studies, Elara practiced the art of meditation. Each morning, she would rise before dawn, finding a quiet spot where she could sit undisturbed. She closed her eyes, inhaled deeply, and envisioned herself back at the stone circle, the heart of her mystical awakening.

Meditation Practice: Grounding in the Mystic's Path

As you sit comfortably, close your eyes and take three deep breaths. With each inhale, imagine drawing in the cool, fresh air of the forest. With each exhale, release any tension or worry. Picture yourself walking through a dense, inviting forest, the ground soft underfoot, the air alive with the energy of nature.

Imagine coming upon a clearing with an ancient stone in the center. As you approach the stone, feel a warm, tingling sensation starting at your feet and moving up through your body. Place your hands upon the stone, feeling its ancient energy pulse into you. Allow this energy to fill you with a sense of purpose and connection.

Hold this image and sensation for a few moments. When you are ready, gently withdraw your hands, and imagine stepping back from the stone, carrying its energy with you. Take three deep breaths and open your eyes, returning to your surroundings with a sense of peace and clarity.

Through these meditative practices, Elara's connection to her mystical path deepened. She felt anchored in her purpose, driven by a force that transcended her previous existence. She knew this was just the beginning, and the path ahead was both daunting and filled with light. The call of the mystic had been answered, and her journey had truly begun.

Chapter 2: The Veil Thins

In the small village of Ealdor, nestled between the whispering forests and the serene waters of Lake Llyr, lived Aeliana, a young woman whose spirit was as wild as the wind that danced through the treetops. From a young age, Aeliana felt a deep, unexplained connection to the unseen world, a pull towards the mysteries that lay beyond the grasp of the ordinary. Her heart thrummed with a longing to understand the whispers of the trees and the secrets of the stars.

As the village prepared for the annual Festival of the Moon, a time when the veil between the physical and spiritual worlds was believed to thin, Aeliana's anticipation grew. She sensed an approaching change, a shift that might finally unveil the purpose of the inexplicable callings she felt.

On the eve of the festival, the villagers gathered around massive bonfires, their faces illuminated by the gentle flames. Stories of ancient gods and mystical creatures were shared with reverence, passed down through generations. Aeliana listened intently, her mind adrift in the tales of the old.

As midnight approached, the high priestess, a venerable woman known as Morwenna, beckoned Aeliana forward. The elders had noticed her deep connection to the mystical realms, and they believed it was her time to undergo the Ritual of the Veil. With a mixture of excitement and apprehension, Aeliana stepped towards the sacred circle, her heart pounding with every step.

The circle was set in a clearing, under the open sky where the stars seemed to converge directly above. Morwenna handed Aeliana a small, silver amulet, shaped like a crescent moon, and whispered, "This has been passed down through the mystics of Ealdor. Tonight, it will reveal your path."

Aeliana clasped the amulet tightly in her hands, feeling its cool surface against her skin. The villagers began to chant in a language that seemed both strange and familiar, their voices rising and falling with the rhythm of the wind. As the chanting intensified, Aeliana closed her eyes and took a deep breath, centering herself in the midst of the swirling energy.

Suddenly, the air around her thickened, and the sounds of the forest amplified—the rustling leaves, the distant call of a night owl, the gentle lap of lake waters against the shore. It was as if the world was breathing with her, aligning with her spirit.

In the sanctuary of her closed eyes, Aeliana saw a vision. She was standing in a lush, verdant forest, the trees towering and ancient, their branches stretching towards the heavens as if in prayer. A path lay before her, dappled with golden sunlight that filtered through the leaves. She began to walk, her feet bare, feeling the cool, soft earth beneath them.

As she walked, the forest seemed to whisper to her, voices of old, guiding her deeper into its heart. She came upon a clearing where a majestic oak stood, its trunk wide and welcoming. At its base, a fox with fur as red as the autumn leaves appeared. It looked at her with knowing eyes, then turned and darted into the underbrush, as if inviting her to follow.

Aeliana pursued the fox through the thicket, her senses heightened, every leaf and twig acutely alive in her perception. The chase led her to a hidden glen where a pool of water mirrored the moon's silvery light. The fox vanished, and in its place stood a woman draped in robes of shimmering blue, her hair flowing like the waters of the pool.

"You have come," the woman said, her voice echoing like a melody. "You are the bridge, Aeliana. The one who will walk between the worlds."

Aeliana's breath caught in her throat. "Who are you?" she asked, her voice barely a whisper.

"I am Arianrhod, goddess of the moon and the tides that govern life. I have watched over you, child of the earth. The veil thins not just in places, but in beings. You are such a being—born to see, to know, to heal."

Tears welled up in Aeliana's eyes as understanding dawned. Her connection to the unseen was not a burden, but a gift—a purpose she was born to fulfill.

Arianrhod stepped closer, laying a hand on Aeliana's shoulder. "Embrace your power. Use it to heal, to guide, to connect. But remember, the path is also one of sacrifice. To see is to know, and to know is to feel, deeply."

With those words, the vision began to fade, and the sounds of the festival slowly crept back into Aeliana's consciousness. She opened her eyes to find the villagers staring at her in awe, Morwenna smiling gently.

"You have crossed the veil," Morwenna said. "Welcome back, Mystic of Ealdor."

As the fire crackled and the stars twinkled above, Aeliana felt a peace settle over her. She now knew her path, her purpose. The journey ahead would be filled with challenges and wonders, but she was ready. With the divine guidance of Arianrhod and the strength of her newfound identity, Aeliana would navigate the seen and unseen worlds, bridging them with her presence, her compassion, and her unwavering spirit.

And as the first light of dawn crept over the horizon, coloring the world in hues of gold and pink, Aeliana felt the veil not just thinning, but welcoming her into the mysteries it held. The journey was just beginning.

Chapter 3: The Ancient Scrolls

In the heart of an old forest, shrouded in the mist of time and mystery, Layla found herself drawn to an abandoned monastery that whispered of olden magic and forgotten truths. As she pushed open the heavy wooden door, it creaked on its hinges, the sound echoing through the empty stone halls like the distant call of an ancient beast. The air was thick with the scent of moss and the parchment of books long unread.

The monastery's library was a cavernous room, with walls lined with towering bookshelves that reached towards the shadowy ceiling. It was here, among these silent sentinels packed with scrolls and tomes bound in leather, that Layla felt the pulsating heart of the place. The dim light filtering through the stained-glass windows cast colorful patterns on the dusty floor, each step she took kicking up small clouds beneath her feet.

Her fingers trailed along the spines of the books, feeling the impressions of titles too faded to read. It was a touch of intuition that stopped her at a particularly unassuming shelf where the wood seemed to hum under her fingers. With a gentle tug, she pulled out a scroll wrapped in deep red ribbon, sealed with a wax emblem of an eye encircled by stars. The seal cracked as she unfurled the scroll, releasing a faint aroma of cedar and lavender, smells that sang of protection and wisdom.

As Layla spread the scroll on a nearby reading table, the script revealed itself in the dancing light—a flowing script that spoke of the ancient mystics, those who had walked the path of divine enlightenment through the shadows of their own souls. The text was a testament to their journeys, their trials, and the esoteric knowledge they had gleaned from the realms that lay beyond the veil.

The first passage caught her breath in her throat:

"In the twilight of the moon's embrace, where shadows dance with the light, the Mystic finds her path. She who seeks the hidden doors must first learn the language of the silent whisper, the murmur of the earth, and the sigh of the stars."

Layla, mesmerized, realized these were not just stories. They were maps—guides to the spiritual realms that few could see and fewer still could traverse. Her heart quickened as she read on, each word a step deeper into the mystic world.

"To the Mystic, the journey inward is the greatest of all explorations. She must shed the veils of illusion cast by the mundane world and peer into the depths of her own soul. There, in the wellspring of her innermost being, lies the echo of the cosmos, waiting to reveal its secrets to those who dare listen."

The scroll detailed meditations, the kind that involved not just sitting and reflecting but actively engaging with the elements. It spoke of midnight walks under the new moon, of collecting dew from leaves at dawn, and of listening to the wind's tales as it swept through desolate valleys. Each act was a ritual, each observation a prayer.

One particular meditation caught Layla's attention—a reflective exercise meant to attune the Mystic's inner rhythm to that of the earth. The instructions were clear:

"Sit beneath the oldest tree you can find just as the sun begins to set. Close your eyes and press your palms against the soil. Breathe deep the scent of earth and decay, of life and death mingled in the air. With each breath, imagine your consciousness sinking deeper into the ground, spreading out like the roots of the tree above you. Listen. What does the earth whisper to you in its ancient language? What secrets does it hold beneath its surface?"

Layla knew exactly the tree the scroll spoke of—a massive oak that stood alone at the crest of a hill, overlooking the valley. It was said to be as old as the monastery itself, perhaps older.

The scroll continued, offering guidance on how to interpret the messages received during these meditations. It wasn't enough to merely listen; understanding the language of the universe required a heart open to the old ways, to the connections between all things.

As the sun dipped below the horizon, casting the library into shadows, Layla rolled up the scroll. Her mind was alight with possibilities, her soul stirred by the call of the Mystic path. There was much to learn, much to explore, and the night was just beginning.

She left the library with the scroll tucked safely under her arm, her steps light, almost floating as she made her way toward the old oak. Tonight, she would begin her true journey into mysticism, guided by the ancient wisdom of those who had walked this path before her. The moon, a slender crescent in the twilight sky, seemed to smile down at her, a silent sentinel to the unfolding mysteries.

As Layla sat beneath the old oak, pressing her palms into the cool soil, the world seemed to hold its breath. The wind whispered through the leaves, carrying with it the faintest echo of voices long forgotten, calling her to join the dance of shadow and light.

And so, under the watchful eye of the crescent moon, Layla began to meditate, her heart open, her mind clear, ready to receive the wisdom of the earth. The journey of the Mystic had begun.

Chapter 4: The Dream Oracle

As Anaya settled into her new, albeit mysterious, life in the secluded village nestled at the foot of Mount Kailasa, her nights began to stir with visions. Dreams, once mere echoes of daily trivialities, transformed into vivid gateways to a realm she could only assume was touched by the divine. Tonight, like many nights before, she prepared for her journey into sleep with more intention than most would for their waking hours.

Anaya sat cross-legged on a woven mat in her modest room, the only light emanating from a single candle, its flame flickering like a hesitant whisper in the quiet night. Around her, the walls were adorned with ancient tapestries that depicted scenes of gods and goddesses, battles between cosmic forces, and serene ascetics in deep meditation. Each figure seemed to pulse with a life of its own under the candle's glow, watching over her as she closed her eyes to meditate.

Her meditation before sleep was a ritual to cleanse her mind, akin to washing one's hands before a meal. She focused on her breathing, each inhale deeper than the last, each exhale a release of the day's worries and mundane thoughts. As her physical world faded, her inner world illuminated, ready to receive the messages from beyond.

Tonight, her subconscious mind prepared to walk the landscapes that the mystics called the Dreamworld - a place where the thin veil between the mundane and the divine was lifted, allowing sacred messages to flow freely.

In the Dream

Anaya found herself in a vast desert under a twilight sky, a blanket of stars her only guide. She walked barefoot, the cool sand comforting her soles, each step creating a soft impression behind her. In the distance, a figure robed in white beckoned her forward.

As she approached, the figure's features became clearer—a woman with eyes as deep and dark as the night sky, her hands open in invitation.

"Welcome, Anaya," the woman's voice was like a melody, harmonious with the whispering winds. "I am Seera, your guide for tonight's revelations."

Anaya bowed slightly, "I am honored, Seera. What wisdom do you share with me in this sacred space?"

Seera smiled warmly, turning to walk alongside Anaya. "The dreams you see are windows to not only your soul but to the truths the universe wishes to unveil. Each vision, each symbol, holds a key to the wisdom you seek."

They stopped before a large, ancient oak tree that stood alone, its branches sprawling wildly against the backdrop of the cosmos. Seera gestured towards the tree, "Look closely, Anaya."

As Anaya peered at the tree, the branches seemed to swirl and dance, forming images and scenes. She saw herself as a child, running through fields; as a young woman, stepping through the gates of the mystical village; and now, as a seeker, standing under the oak tree.

"These are your past, present, and future," Seera explained. "The tree is the Tree of Life, its branches represent the paths of your destiny. Some branches intertwine, others stand alone, but all are connected to the same roots, much like the interconnectedness of all beings."

Anaya watched, fascinated as the scenes shifted, revealing deeper, more esoteric layers. One showed her an old book, its pages fluttering open as if caught in a gentle breeze, the script too ancient for her to understand.

"This book," Seera said, noticing Anaya's intrigue, "holds the knowledge of the mystics before you. In your waking life, seek this tome, for it contains guidance for your journey ahead."

The vision faded, and the tree stilled, its branches now silent and solemn under the starlit sky.

"Remember, Anaya, that the wisdom of the Dream Oracle is profound but often shrouded in mystery. It is not merely about seeing but understanding and integrating these visions into your life," Seera's voice echoed as the dream began to dissolve.

Awakening

Anaya's eyes fluttered open to the familiar darkness of her room. The candle had long burned out, leaving behind a faint trace of smoke that danced upwards in the still air. Her heart was full, her mind alight with the vivid imagery and cryptic messages of her dream.

She reached for the journal she kept by her side, a habit she had formed since her dreams had turned prophetic. With a steady hand, she penned down every detail she could recall—the desert, the oak tree, the ancient book, and Seera's wise words. Each word she wrote was a step towards deciphering the deeper meanings, a commitment to the path laid out by the Dream Oracle.

As the night waned and dawn approached, Anaya sat in contemplation, her spirit intertwined with the mystic energies that coursed through her veins. She knew that the journey was not just about seeking the truth but about living it, each day a step closer to her true destiny as a mystic.

The lessons of the Dream Oracle were clear: listen, understand, and integrate. Anaya felt a profound connection to something greater than herself, a part of a grand tapestry of existence that was both humbling and empowering.

As the first light of dawn crept through her window, casting soft golden hues across her room, Anaya felt renewed. Armed with the insights from her dreams and the guidance of Seera, she was ready to face the challenges of her mystical journey, each step guided by the wisdom of the dreams that visited her in the silence of the night.

Chapter 5: The Ritual of Silence

In the mystical journey of Eleora, a young seeker touched by the divine, the fifth chapter of her enlightenment came upon a night painted with the starless ink of a new moon. The village elders had spoken of the Ritual of Silence, a sacred practice observed once every decade, where silence was not merely the absence of sound, but a profound gateway to the deeper realms of existence. Eleora, with her heart as curious as the endless sky, decided to embark on this ancient path to harness the whispers of the universe.

As she approached the Temple of Whispered Truths, the air grew thick with a palpable sense of anticipation. The temple stood solemn and majestic, its ancient stones etched with the passage of countless seasons. It was said that within its walls, one could hear the heartbeat of the earth if one listened closely enough.

The high priestess, a venerable woman named Seraphine, greeted Eleora at the temple's entrance. With eyes as deep as the cosmos, she handed Eleora a simple, unadorned robe. "To enter the silence, you must first shed the noise of the world," Seraphine whispered, her voice a gentle breeze in the quiet of the night.

Eleora changed into the robe, feeling its weight as a comforting embrace that connected her to the countless seekers who had walked this path before. She followed Seraphine into the heart of the temple, where a circular room awaited, illuminated only by the soft glow of moonlight filtering through a single window.

"Here," Seraphine said as she gestured to the center of the room, "you will sit, you will listen, and most importantly, you will be silent. The Ritual of Silence is not merely about refraining from speech but about listening with all of you—your heart, your soul, your essence."

Eleora took her place on the cold stone floor, crossing her legs and resting her hands lightly on her knees. Seraphine lit several incense sticks, their smoke swirling into the air, carrying prayers and intentions upwards. As the last echoes of movement faded away, Seraphine left, and the door closed with a hush, sealing Eleora inside.

The silence descended like a cloak. At first, it was merely the absence of sound, but as minutes turned into hours, it deepened, growing layers, textures, and colors. Eleora's initial discomfort with the stillness gave way to a burgeoning sense of peace. The beating of her heart became a steady drum, grounding her to the moment, to the earth beneath her, to the very fabric of her being.

As the night progressed, the silence spoke. It whispered of ancient times, of the laughter and tears of those who had walked the earth before. It roared with the winds of change that had sculpted mountains and carved rivers. It sang with the voices of the stars, distant yet familiar. Eleora listened, truly listened, and in doing so, she heard not just the world but also herself.

She confronted her fears—shadowy figures that danced at the edges of her consciousness. She embraced her hopes, bright and bold, pulsing with the promise of tomorrow. The silence was no longer empty but filled with the music of her soul, a symphony of light and darkness, of being and non-being.

As dawn approached, painting the sky with strokes of pink and gold, Eleora felt a shift within her. The silence had changed her; it had carved out spaces within her being, making room for wisdom and understanding. She understood now that silence was not the absence of noise but the presence of an infinite universe whispering the secrets of existence.

When Seraphine returned, the temple was awash with the gentle light of morning. She found Eleora not as the girl who had entered but as a seeker transformed by the sacred silence. With a knowing smile, Seraphine helped Eleora to her feet.

"The voices of the universe have spoken through the silence," Seraphine said, her voice a reflection of the peace that enveloped them. "Carry their whispers in your heart, for they are the keys to the mysteries of life."

As Eleora stepped out of the temple, the world greeted her with the familiar sounds of morning—birds chirping, leaves rustling, the distant calls of the waking village. Yet, these sounds were no longer just noises; they were part of the larger symphony of existence, each note a thread in the tapestry of the cosmos.

The Ritual of Silence had ended, but for Eleora, the journey into the mystic realms of understanding and connection had just begun. She walked forward, each step a silent prayer, each breath a silent song, forever changed, forever attuned to the divine silence that spoke louder than any word ever could.

Chapter 6: The Sacred Grove

In the heart of a forgotten forest, where the trees whispered secrets older than time, Mariah found the path that few mortals would ever tread. It was a path carpeted with lush moss and dappled sunlight, beckoning her deeper into its embrace. She had been told of the Sacred Grove, a place where the spirits of nature communed and shared their ancient wisdom with those who dared to listen.

Mariah's journey to the Sacred Grove began at dawn, as the first light of the sun painted the world in hues of gold and amber. The air was cool and fresh, filled with the scent of earth and wildflowers. With each step, the worries of the mundane world fell away, replaced by a growing sense of anticipation and awe.

As she walked, Mariah reflected on her journey so far. The path of a mystic was not an easy one. It demanded courage, faith, and the willingness to face the unknown. But it was also a path of incredible beauty and profound connection. Every experience, every challenge, was an opportunity to delve deeper into the mysteries of existence.

Finally, after what seemed like hours of walking, Mariah arrived at the edge of the Sacred Grove. The air here was different—thicker, almost palpable, as if charged with an unseen energy. The trees stood tall and majestic, their branches interlocking overhead to form a natural cathedral.

Mariah stepped into the grove with reverence. The moment her feet touched the sacred ground, a hush fell over the forest. The usual sounds of rustling leaves and chirping birds ceased, and in their place, a deep, resonant silence enveloped her.

She walked to the center of the grove, where an ancient stone altar lay. It was covered in moss and surrounded by a circle of stones, each one engraved with symbols that seemed to glow faintly in the forest's muted light.

Mariah closed her eyes and took a deep breath, grounding herself in the present moment. She reached out with her senses, feeling the energy of the grove pulsating around her. It was a gentle, nurturing presence, ancient and wise.

Opening her eyes, Mariah began the Ritual of Communion, a sacred practice passed down through generations of mystics. She lit a small fire on the altar, using herbs and woods gathered from the forest. The smoke rose in thin spirals, carrying her prayers to the spirits of the grove.

"Guardians of the Sacred Grove," she whispered, her voice steady and clear. "I come in search of wisdom and guidance. I am a seeker on the path of the mystic, and I ask for your blessing and your teachings."

As the last word left her lips, the air around her shimmered, and the silence was broken by a soft, melodious voice. "Welcome, child of the earth," it said, resonating through the grove like the gentle hum of the earth itself. "Your journey has led you here, and we have been awaiting you."

Mariah looked around, trying to locate the source of the voice, but saw no one. She realized then that the spirits were speaking to her through the very essence of the grove itself.

"We are the spirits of nature, the ancient ones who have guarded this sacred place through the ages," the voice continued. "We have watched you approach with a heart full of sincerity and a soul yearning for connection. What is it that you seek, Mariah?"

Mariah took a moment to gather her thoughts. "I seek understanding," she replied. "In my heart, I feel a deep connection to the world around me, to the earth, the sky, and all living things. But I struggle to understand the depth of this connection and how to use it to help others."

The fire on the altar flared brightly for a moment, and warmth spread through Mariah's body. "To understand your connection to all things, you must first understand yourself," the voice said gently. "You are a part of the web of life, woven into it as surely as the trees and the stars. Your spirit is a spark of the divine, and your actions ripple through the world like waves on a pond."

The voice paused, and the air filled with a soft, golden light. "Sit, child, and meditate with us. Let the energy of the grove fill you, teach you, guide you."

Mariah did as instructed, sitting cross-legged on the ground before the altar. She closed her eyes and focused on her breathing, letting the serene energy of the grove wash over her. As she meditated, visions began to form in her mind's eye. She saw the earth from above, a beautiful, vibrant tapestry of colors and life. She saw the connections between all things, invisible threads that bound the world together in a complex, beautiful pattern.

She saw herself as a part of that tapestry, a thread woven tightly into the fabric of existence. She felt a profound sense of peace and understanding, a realization that she was never alone, for she was connected to the infinite.

When Mariah opened her eyes, the grove was bathed in the soft light of twilight. The fire on the altar had burned down to embers, and the air was once again filled with the sounds of the forest. She stood, feeling renewed and filled with a deep, unshakeable peace.

"Thank you," she whispered to the spirits, her voice full of gratitude. "I will carry your wisdom with me."

As she walked back through the forest, the path lit by the gentle light of the setting sun, Mariah knew that her journey was far from over. But she also knew that she carried with her the blessings of the Sacred Grove, and the wisdom of the spirits who dwelled there. And with that knowledge, she walked forward into the twilight, ready to face whatever the path of the mystic might bring.

Chapter 7: The Mystic's Challenge

As the first light of dawn painted the horizon with hues of orange and pink, Elara felt the familiar stirrings of apprehension mixed with excitement. Today was the day she would face the Mystic's Challenge, a pivotal trial that every aspirant of the mystical arts had to endure. It was said that the challenge would not only test one's mystical abilities but also one's faith in the unseen forces of the universe.

Elara had spent the previous night in meditation, seeking guidance and strength from the Goddess of the Mystics, a deity known for her wisdom and connection to the higher realms. The goddess had appeared in Elara's dreams, her presence both calming and empowering, whispering that the path ahead, though fraught with obstacles, was one that Elara was ready to tread.

The Mystic's Challenge was held in the ancient ruins of Solena, a place believed to be charged with potent spiritual energy. It was here that the veils between the physical world and the etheric planes were thinnest, allowing for profound mystical experiences. As Elara approached the ruins, the air seemed to hum with energy, the stones underfoot vibrating with ancient power.

At the center of the ruins stood the Altar of Trials, a stone table surrounded by statues of the past mystics who had shaped the path of their craft. It was here that Elara's challenge would commence. The elders of the mystical community, cloaked in robes of midnight blue, gathered around the altar, their eyes bearing the weight of wisdom and knowledge.

"Elara, you have come to face the Mystic's Challenge," the High Mystic began, her voice echoing slightly in the open air. "This trial will confront you not only with external adversities but will also plunge you into the depths of your own psyche. Are you prepared to face what lies within and without?"

Elara nodded, her resolve firm. "I am ready."

With a solemn nod, the High Mystic gestured to the altar where a series of ancient relics lay. These items were to be used by Elara to overcome the trials: a crystal for clarity, a feather for lightness of being, and a vial of sacred water for purification.

The first trial began. Elara was to use the crystal to navigate through a labyrinth that had been outlined with stones on the ground. As she entered the labyrinth, her mind began to fill with doubts and fears, each step forward intensifying her inner turmoil. Whispering a prayer to the Goddess, Elara focused on the crystal, which glowed softly in her hand, its light guiding her through the winding paths.

After what felt like an eternity, she emerged at the heart of the labyrinth, a small clearing where a single flower bloomed—an orchid radiant in the morning light. It was a symbol of her success in overcoming her doubts, and Elara felt a surge of relief and pride.

The second trial was the trial of air, where Elara had to scale a cliff face to retrieve a scroll placed at the summit. This tested her physical limits and her ability to maintain a calm and focused mind in the face of fear. Using the feather, she lightened her body, making her movements graceful and effortless. As she reached the summit, her hands trembling as she took the scroll, she realized the power of lightness in overcoming physical boundaries.

The final trial was perhaps the most daunting. Elara was to enter the Cave of Shadows, a place said to manifest one's deepest fears and insecurities. Armed with the vial of sacred water, she stepped into the darkness, her heart pounding in her chest.

Inside, shadows danced along the walls, morphing into figures and faces from her past—voices of doubt, criticism, and fear that she had long buried. With each step, the voices grew louder, urging her to turn back. But Elara pressed forward, opening the vial of sacred water and allowing its purity to cleanse the space around her. As the water touched the ground, the voices began to dissipate, replaced by a profound silence.

Emerging from the cave, Elara was met with the smiles and approving nods of the elders. She had passed the Mystic's Challenge, proving not only her ability to wield mystical tools but also her strength in confronting and overcoming her inner darkness.

As the ceremony concluded, the High Mystic approached Elara, placing a medallion around her neck—an emblem of her success and her readiness to advance further in her mystical studies.

"The challenges you faced today were reflections of life's greater trials," the High Mystic explained. "You have shown great courage and wisdom. Remember, the true mystic's path is never free from obstacles, but it is how you navigate these obstacles that defines your journey."

Elara felt a deep sense of accomplishment and clarity. She knew that this was merely the beginning of her mystical journey, but now she was armed with the knowledge that she had the strength to face whatever lay ahead.

As the sun climbed higher into the sky, casting a golden light over the ruins of Solena, Elara felt a profound connection to the mystics who had walked this path before her. She was ready for the next chapter of her journey, emboldened by the trials she had overcome and curious about the mysteries that awaited her discovery.

Chapter 8: The Alchemical Marriage

As the sun began its descent, casting long shadows over the sacred grove, Aria found herself walking slowly towards the ancient stone circle that had stood as a witness to countless rites and ceremonies of the mystics before her. She was here to undertake one of the most profound rituals known to those who walked the mystical path—the Alchemical Marriage, the sacred union of the masculine and feminine energies within, aiming for spiritual wholeness and harmony.

The air was cool, carrying the scent of pine and earth, grounding and centering her as she moved. Around her, the forest seemed to hold its breath, the usually chattering birds silent, as if in respect for the gravity of her undertaking.

Aria had spent months preparing for this moment, learning to recognize and balance the dual aspects of her nature. She understood that the divine masculine within her spoke in the language of logic, action, and assertiveness, while the divine feminine whispered of intuition, empathy, and receptiveness. Her guide, an elderly mystic named Mael, had taught her that true power lay in balancing these forces, not allowing one to dominate the other.

As she reached the center of the stone circle, she saw Mael waiting for her, a gentle smile playing on his lips. He was clad in a robe that shimmered with the hues of twilight, his wise eyes reflecting the deep knowledge of the ancients.

"Are you ready, Aria?" he asked, his voice as soft as the breeze that rustled through the leaves.

"I am," she replied, her voice steady despite the butterflies dancing in her stomach.

Mael nodded and stepped aside, gesturing her towards the altar at the center of the circle. On it lay symbols of the masculine and feminine: a sturdy oak branch and a delicate silver cup.

"Tonight, you will engage in the Alchemical Marriage, a ritual that will help you embrace and unite the dual aspects of your being. This is not just a merging but an acceptance, an understanding that both energies are essential and must be honored equally," Mael explained.

Aria took a deep breath and approached the altar. She picked up the oak branch and the silver cup, feeling the weight and texture of each. As instructed, she placed them side by side, symbolizing the initial acknowledgment of each energy's presence within her.

Mael began chanting in an ancient tongue, his voice rising and falling with the rhythm of the earth itself. Aria closed her eyes and began her meditation, visualizing the oak branch and silver cup within her. She saw them not as separate entities but as complementary, each giving strength to the other.

In her mind's eye, the branch wrapped around the cup, protecting and supporting it, while the cup filled the spaces between the branch's leaves, offering nourishment and care. Gradually, the images began to merge, forming a new symbol—a tree with leaves of silver and branches that flowed like water.

As the visualization grew clearer, Aria felt a warmth spreading through her chest, a sense of peace and power filling her being. She realized that for too long, she had struggled with internal conflicts, one part of her always trying to suppress or overcome the other. Now, she felt a harmony she had never known, a sense of being complete and balanced.

Mael's voice brought her back to the physical world. "The Alchemical Marriage is complete within you, Aria. You have embraced both your strengths and your vulnerabilities. This balance will guide you in your journey forward, allowing you to act with wisdom and compassion."

As the ritual concluded, Aria opened her eyes. The stones around her seemed to glow in the moonlight, and she felt an indescribable connection to everything around her—the stones, the trees, the very sky above.

In the days that followed, Aria noticed a change in how she approached her mystical studies and interactions.

With her energies in balance, she could assert herself when necessary but also listen and respond with empathy.

Her decision-making was no longer a tug-of-war between competing impulses but a harmonious dialogue within her soul.

The Alchemical Marriage had transformed her, not by changing who she was, but by revealing the depth of her own nature. She moved through the world with a new ease, her steps sure and her heart open.

As Aria continued her journey, she often returned to the lessons of that night. She learned that maintaining balance was an ongoing process, requiring attention and care.

Each day offered new challenges and opportunities to apply the wisdom of the Alchemical Marriage.

 And in each challenge, Aria found not just obstacles but stepping stones, leading her ever onward on her path as a mystic.

Chapter 9: The Chalice of Visions

In the mystical journey of Liora, the protagonist, her next encounter was with the ancient and mysterious Chalice of Visions. This sacred object, whispered about in the elder mystics' tales, was said to hold the power to reveal not just the future, but also the many possible pathways one's life could take, manifesting potential realities as vivid as waking dreams.

Liora had journeyed far, through shadowed forests and over sunlit hills, to reach the Temple of Ghal Maraz, where the Chalice was kept. The temple stood solitary atop a high plateau, surrounded by clouds that shimmered with ethereal light. It was a place out of time, seldom touched by the hands of the mortal world.

As she approached the temple's massive stone doors, they opened with a sound like the sigh of the wind, revealing a hall lit by candles that burned with silver flames. The air inside was heavy with the scent of incense and old magic. Liora's heart beat with excitement and a touch of fear—the good kind of fear that spoke of approaching the heart of a deep mystery.

Walking through the hall, her footsteps echoed off the stone, a lonely sound that reminded her of her solitary path. At the end of the hall stood an altar, and upon it, cradled by a nest of moonlight beams, was the Chalice of Visions. It was smaller than she had imagined, simple in form but exquisite, made of a crystal that pulsed softly with inner light.

Liora approached the altar and reached out slowly. As her fingers brushed the chalice, a surge of energy shot through her, and her mind's eye was flung wide open. She saw herself in countless forms and situations: Liora as a healer, her hands glowing with life; Liora as a sage, surrounded by eager pupils; Liora as a wanderer, exploring realms that no maps had ever charted.

The vision shifted, and she was in the depths of the ocean, her body adapting to the water as if born to it, speaking with creatures whose language was song and current. Another shift, and she was in a desert, her skin baked by the sun, her feet tracing the patterns of ancient dances in the sand for rain.

As the visions poured through her, Liora remained anchored in the reality of the temple by the weight of the Chalice in her hands. Each vision felt like a life she could live, each choice a path she could follow. It was overwhelming and exhilarating.

When the flow of visions finally slowed, Liora set the Chalice down gently. She took several deep breaths, grounding herself with the cool stone beneath her palms. The experience had not just shown her what could be—it had expanded her understanding of what it meant to be alive, to be part of the weave of the world.

Now, the time came for the meditation that would help integrate these visions into her conscious understanding and wisdom. She sat cross-legged before the altar, closed her eyes, and began to breathe deeply, evenly.

In her meditation, Liora envisioned herself walking down a path in a lush forest. Each step she took represented a choice, each turn a decision. She saw the paths branch off around her, each one a different color, glowing with the light of possibility. She took a step down a path bathed in blue light, the color of depth and intuition.

As she walked, she focused on the feeling of each potential life she might lead. Some paths felt warm and inviting, others cold and challenging. She understood that each path had its lessons, its hardships, and its joys. The meditation allowed her to explore these paths without commitment, understanding deeply that her choices would shape her destiny, but also that there was no 'wrong' path—only different experiences.

The meditation taught her to embrace the uncertainty and the multiple possibilities that life offered. It showed her how to hold lightly to one path while acknowledging the existence of others. She learned to walk her chosen path with commitment, yet keep her heart open to change and new directions.

After what felt like hours, Liora opened her eyes. She felt a profound sense of peace and a newfound confidence in her ability to choose her path wisely, guided by the deep inner knowledge that the Chalice of Visions had awakened within her.

Rising from her meditation, Liora filled the Chalice with water from a small, clear stream that trickled through the temple. She drank deeply, the water cool and sweet on her tongue, sealing her experiences and insights within her.

As she left the temple, the Chalice of Visions once again nestled on its altar, Liora felt changed. She was more herself than she had ever been, yet she was also more than she had been before. She carried within her the knowledge of infinite potential and the wisdom to navigate it. Her journey was far from over, but she moved forward with a new understanding, her heart and mind open to whatever paths might unfold before her.

Chapter 10: The Hermit's Path

As the sun dipped below the horizon, casting a cloak of twilight across the land, Eliana found herself walking along a narrow, winding path that led away from the bustling life of her village. The path was known to few, and those who knew it seldom spoke of where it led. But for Eliana, the path was a calling, a silent whisper that had grown louder with each passing day, urging her towards solitude, towards the profound silence of the Hermit's Path.

For weeks, Eliana had felt an overwhelming desire to retreat from the world she knew, to delve deeper into her own soul, and to confront the mysteries that awaited her in the solitude of the wilderness. Her mystical experiences had opened her eyes to realms beyond the ordinary, and now, they called her to explore the inner sanctum of her being.

The village shaman had once told her, "In solitude, you find the orchestra of your soul playing the symphony of the divine." These words echoed in her mind as she stepped further away from the familiar and into the embrace of the unknown.

As night fell, Eliana reached the heart of a dense forest where ancient trees stood like sentinels, their branches whispering secrets of the old ways. She set up a small camp by a clearing and lit a fire that flickered with a comforting glow against the encroaching darkness. Sitting by the fire, she took a deep breath, inhaling the earthy aroma of the forest, and allowed the quiet of the night to envelop her.

The first night passed in profound silence. Eliana meditated by the fire, focusing on her breath, letting each inhalation draw in peace and each exhalation release any remnants of worldly concerns. The crackling of the fire seemed to synchronize with her heartbeat, creating a meditative harmony that calmed her spirit.

In the days that followed, Eliana embraced the Hermit's Path with dedication. She rose with the sun and meditated, her mind slowly shedding the cacophony of unnecessary thoughts, layer by layer. She wandered through the forest, her bare feet treading softly on the mossy earth, attuned to the subtle life around her. Birds sang from the treetops, and the wind carried the scent of wildflowers and pine.

One morning, while walking through a particularly dense part of the forest, Eliana stumbled upon an old, moss-covered stone that bore enigmatic symbols. Recognizing the symbols from the ancient scrolls she had studied, she realized this stone was a marker, a guidepost used by ancient mystics who had walked this path before her.

Eliana spent hours each day sitting by the stone, tracing the symbols with her fingers, and meditating on their meanings. As she did, visions began to form in her mind's eye. She saw flashes of ancient ceremonies, heard the echoes of old prayers, and felt the presence of the mystics who had once sought solace in these woods. These visions were not mere figments of imagination; they were the spiritual heritage of the Hermit's Path, passed down through the silent communion of soul to soul.

As the days turned into weeks, Eliana's sense of self expanded. The solitude did not bring loneliness but a profound connection to all life. She realized that in silence, she was not alone but deeply connected to the web of life that pulsated through the forest. The trees, the stones, the flowing streams, and the scurrying animals—all spoke to her in the language of silence, a language her heart understood perfectly.

In her solitude, Eliana also confronted her inner shadows. Fears that she had suppressed, insecurities she had hidden, all surfaced in the quiet moments of introspection. With each confrontation, she practiced a meditation of acceptance and release. She visualized her fears as leaves floating down a gentle stream, acknowledged them, and let them go, allowing the waters to carry them away.

One particularly starry night, as Eliana sat by her campfire, a profound peace settled over her. She realized that the journey of the mystic was not to escape life but to penetrate its mysteries deeply and return with wisdom to share. The Hermit's Path was not just a physical journey but an inner pilgrimage to the sanctuary of the soul.

As dawn broke, painting the sky with hues of pink and gold, Eliana knew it was time to return to her village. She packed her few belongings and took one last look at the clearing that had been her home. The fire was out, but its warmth lingered in her heart.

With every step back towards her village, Eliana felt a new sense of purpose. The solitude had changed her; the silence had spoken to her more eloquently than any voice ever could. She returned not as a woman who had fled from the world, but as a mystic who had embraced the solitude and found within it the eternal dance of life and spirit.

Her return was quiet, unnoticed by many, but the change within her was profound. In the days and months that followed, Eliana shared her experiences with those who sought her wisdom, teaching them the meditations and the lessons of the Hermit's Path. She became a beacon of light, a testament to the transformative power of solitude and the enduring call of the mystic's journey.

Chapter 11: The Portal of Stars

Under the vast expanse of the night sky, with a moon that seemed to hang like a glistening pendant, Elara stood at the edge of the world she knew. She had come to this sacred clearing many nights, but tonight was different; tonight, she intended to open the Portal of Stars.

The air was thick with anticipation, a hush settled over the forest as if the trees themselves were holding their breath, waiting for something momentous to occur. Elara took a deep breath, grounding herself in the earth beneath her feet, feeling the connection to all that was, and all that would ever be. The ancient texts had brought her here, to this forgotten grove, where the veil between the dimensions was thinnest.

As she prepared to begin the ritual, Elara recalled the words of the High Mystic, her mentor. "When you are ready, the Portal will open. But remember, child, it is not just about readiness of the mind, but of the heart and soul."

Elara knelt and placed the five sacred stones in a circle around her, each one meticulously chosen for its alignment with the celestial energies. She lit a small fire in the center, the flames flickering and casting ghostly shadows. The fire was essential; it represented light and knowledge, a beacon in the darkness, a guide for the spirits she hoped to commune with tonight.

She closed her eyes and began to chant the ancient incantation, her voice a soft melody that wove through the night air, intertwining with the whispers of the universe. The words were old, older than the mountains, passed down through generations of mystics who had walked this path before her.

As Elara chanted, the sky began to change. The stars seemed to dance, drawing closer, swirling above her in a mesmerizing display of cosmic splendor. The Portal was responding.

"O spirits of the cosmos, hear my call. I seek the wisdom of the ages, the knowledge held within the stars. Let the boundaries between our worlds dissolve. Let me walk among the heavens, if only for a moment."

The ground beneath her vibrated softly, as if the earth itself was humming in tune with her request. A gentle wind picked up, swirling around her, caressing her face like an old friend.

And then, it happened.

Above her, the stars aligned, forming a shimmering gateway, an archway of celestial light that pulsed with otherworldly energy. The Portal of Stars had opened.

Elara stood, her heart pounding with a mix of fear and exhilaration. She stepped forward, entering the Portal. The world around her changed instantly. She was no longer in the forest but was now standing on what seemed to be a pathway of stars. They glimmered underfoot, each step she took resonated with light and sound, a symphony of the universe.

She walked the starlit path, each step revealing flashes of visions and knowledge. Scenes of ancient civilizations that had once looked up at these same stars, mystics and philosophers who had pondered the same eternal questions, all were connected in the vast tapestry of cosmic existence.

As she journeyed further, she encountered spirits of the past; great thinkers and seers who shared whispers of wisdom with her. They spoke of the interconnectedness of all life, the cycles of the universe, and the small but significant role each being played in the grand design.

One spirit, a wise old woman cloaked in starlight, approached Elara. "The wisdom of the stars is the wisdom of connection, of understanding your place in the infinite. You are a child of the cosmos, born of stardust and destined to return to it. Carry this knowledge back to your world, and let it guide you in the dance of life."

Elara listened, her soul absorbing every word, every shimmering truth. It was overwhelming, yet profoundly simple. She was, they all were, part of something far greater than themselves.

As the dawn began to break in the world she had left behind, the Portal of Stars began to fade. Elara knew it was time to return. She walked back along the starlit path, each step taking her closer to her own reality. Stepping out of the Portal, back into the forest clearing, the first light of morning kissed her face. The stones around her lay silent, the fire reduced to embers. But inside her, a fire of a different kind burned—a fire kindled with the wisdom of the stars.

Elara knew her journey was far from over. This experience was but a chapter in her life's book, one that would influence many chapters to come. As she packed her things and prepared to leave the clearing, she felt a profound sense of gratitude and purpose. The universe was vast, and she was but a small part of it, yet she had touched the eternal, and it had changed her forever. With a final glance at the sky, now light with the promise of a new day, Elara stepped forward into her life, ready to share the wisdom of the stars, ready to embrace her role in the cosmic dance.

Chapter 12: The Healing Waters

Lila had always been drawn to the healing aspects of nature, but nothing prepared her for the mystical powers of the legendary Aquarius Spring. Hidden deep within the heart of the ancient forest, the spring was said to possess waters that could heal not just the body, but also the soul. As Lila embarked on her journey to find these mysterious waters, her heart thumped with a mixture of excitement and apprehension. Her path was guided by ancient symbols and whispers of the past, each step taking her deeper into her own mystical journey.

The forest around her was alive with the sounds of nature; birds chirping harmoniously and the wind whispering through the leaves. The light filtered through the canopy in golden beams, casting magical patterns on the forest floor. As she walked, Lila felt as though she was stepping through a veil, entering a world that bridged the mundane and the divine. This was the realm of the mystic, where every element of nature held deeper meanings and powers.

After hours of trekking, Lila arrived at a clearing where the air felt charged with a palpable energy. In the center lay the Aquarius Spring, its waters clear and shimmering under the afternoon sun. Surrounding the spring were stones engraved with ancient runes, their meanings long forgotten by time but still holding the energy of their sacred intentions. Lila approached slowly, a sense of reverence washing over her. She knew these waters were sacred, touched by the divine essence of the mystic goddesses.

She knelt by the spring, her fingers lightly touching the surface of the water. It rippled gently under her touch, cool and inviting. Closing her eyes, Lila took a deep breath and prepared herself for the meditation she had learned from the scrolls of the ancient mystics.

Meditation: Water Healing

Lila began her meditation by visualizing the water's energy as a vibrant blue light, radiating purity and healing properties. She imagined this light entering her body through her fingertips, spreading slowly through her veins, calming her mind and healing her spirit. She breathed in sync with the flow of the water, each breath deeper and more calming than the last.

"Water, sacred and pure, I seek your healing. Wash away the ailments of my body and the shadows of my soul. Merge your sacred essence with mine, and make me whole," she whispered.

As she meditated, Lila felt the boundaries between herself and the water blur. The energy of the spring seemed to pulse in rhythm with her heartbeat, and she could feel her ailments, her worries, and her fears washing away, carried off by the sacred waters. This was the healing she had journeyed so far to find, the mystical union of nature and spirit that the mystic goddesses had promised.

After what felt like an eternity, Lila slowly opened her eyes. The world seemed brighter, the colors of the forest more vivid, and the sounds sharper. She knew something profound had changed within her. She had drunk from the wellspring of mystical knowledge and been reborn through its healing waters.

Rising to her feet, Lila filled a small vial with the water from the spring, sealing it with a stopper. This vial would be her talisman, a reminder of the healing and transformation she had experienced. She placed it around her neck, feeling its cool weight against her chest.

With a heart full of gratitude, Lila began her journey back through the forest. The path seemed easier now, as if the forest itself was guiding her steps. She realized that the healing she had experienced was not just about curing physical or emotional pain but about a deeper, spiritual restoration. She had tapped into the ancient wisdom of the mystic goddesses, who taught that true healing comes from understanding and aligning with the divine forces of nature.

As Lila emerged from the forest, the sun was setting, casting the sky in hues of orange and pink. She paused to watch the sunset, feeling a profound connection to the world around her. Her journey to the Aquarius Spring had been a physical one, but the journey within herself was far more significant. She had embraced the mystic path, found healing in the sacred waters, and awakened a deeper part of her soul.

And as the stars began to twinkle in the twilight sky, Lila knew that this was just the beginning. The path of the mystic was long and filled with challenges, but it was also rich with wonders and moments of profound beauty. She was ready to continue her journey, wherever it might lead, with the healing waters of the Aquarius Spring flowing through her, a perpetual source of strength and renewal.

Chapter 13: The Shadow Dance

In the tranquil heart of the forest, where the trees whispered ancient secrets to those who dared listen, Ariadne found herself at a crossroads. It was a place both literal and metaphorical, marked by an ancient stone with runes barely visible under the moss that clung to its surface. She had come here on the guidance of a dream, one that had been recurring with increasing intensity, a dream of dancing shadows and whispering spirits.

As the sun dipped below the horizon, painting the sky in hues of orange and purple, Ariadne sat at the base of the stone, her fingers tracing the runes. Each symbol pulsed under her touch, as if alive with stories waiting to be told. She closed her eyes, taking a deep breath, preparing herself for the night's undertaking—a ritual that would confront her with her deepest fears and unacknowledged desires: the Shadow Dance.

The Shadow Dance was more than a ritual; it was a rite of passage that had been passed down through generations of mystics. It was said that to dance with one's shadow was to understand the true essence of one's soul, to embrace all that was hidden in darkness and bring it into the light.

As darkness enveloped the forest, Ariadne lit a circle of candles around her, each flicker casting soft glows against the darkness, creating a boundary between the known and the unknown. She began the ritual with a chant, an invocation of protection and clarity. Her voice melded with the night sounds, a symphony of frogs croaking and leaves rustling in the gentle breeze.

"Spirits of the forest, keepers of the ancient wisdom, guide me through the darkness, help me face the shadows with courage and grace," she intoned, her voice steady despite the quickening of her heart.

With the chant complete, she rose to her feet, her body starting to move slowly, arms swaying, feet stepping rhythmically on the earth. As she danced, her mind began to clear, thoughts of the day's worries and mundane concerns slipping away like silken scarves in the wind. The dance became more intense, more purposeful. Shadows emerged from the edges of the candlelit circle, figures of dark and light, dancing along with her.

These were the aspects of herself she had long ignored or suppressed—a younger self filled with unresolved anger, a voiceless entity embodying her fears, a proud figure representing her hidden pride. One by one, they joined her in the dance, moving to a rhythm that seemed ancient and sacred.

Ariadne's heart raced as she faced each shadow, not with the intent to banish them, but to understand and integrate them. She remembered the teachings of her mentors: "To deny one's shadow is to deny half of one's soul. Embrace it, and you embrace your whole self."

As she danced, she whispered to each shadow, acknowledging its presence, its right to exist. "I see you, I accept you," she murmured to the figure of anger, its edges blurring and softening in response. "I hear you, I will not silence you," she assured the voiceless shadow, which seemed to gain substance and voice as she spoke.

The dance continued for what seemed like hours, each moment stretching into eternity. Ariadne felt sweat beading her forehead, her limbs heavy but invigorated by the profound encounters. With each acceptance, the shadows grew less intimidating, more a part of her. They danced not against her but with her, in a harmony that felt both empowering and humbling.

As the final shadow, a regal figure of pride, melded back into her form, the forest seemed to sigh, a breeze sweeping through the trees, rustling the leaves in soft applause. Ariadne slowed her dance, eventually stopping, standing still in the center of her candle circle, breathing heavily, feeling a sense of wholeness she had never known before.

She fell to her knees, overwhelmed by emotion. Tears streamed down her cheeks, not of sadness, but of release and relief. "Thank you," she whispered into the night, her voice a blend of fatigue and joy. "Thank you for the dance, for the understanding, for the integration."

As dawn crept over the horizon, the first light of the sun peeking through the trees, Ariadne extinguished the candles. The shadows were gone, integrated into her being, part of her dance not just in this ritual but in life itself. She felt renewed, as if reborn into a world that held no fear of darkness, for she had danced with her shadows and found them not enemies, but allies.

With a newfound strength and a profound sense of peace, Ariadne walked out of the forest, the runes on the ancient stone glowing faintly in the morning light, a silent testament to the power of the Shadow Dance. As she glanced back, the path behind her seemed less daunting, the forest less foreboding. Ahead lay new challenges, new dances, and she faced them not as a woman fragmented by her fears and desires, but as a mystic whole and harmonious within her own depths.

The Shadow Dance had taught her that the darkest parts of ourselves hold the deepest wisdom. In embracing them, we do not just dance the dance of mystics; we dance the dance of life, fully, bravely, beautifully.

Chapter 14: The Circle of Elders

The forest was deep and ancient, its trees standing like sentinels of time. Lara walked through the dense woods, each step deliberate and silent, as though she feared waking the spirits that slumbered beneath the moss-covered earth. Her heart beat in rhythm with the distant sound of a ceremonial drum, a sound that seemed both within and beyond this world. Tonight was the night she was destined to meet the Circle of Elders, a clandestine gathering of mystics who held the keys to esoteric knowledge that had been preserved for millennia.

As she approached the clearing, the trees seemed to part, forming a natural pathway that led to a circle of stones. In the center, a fire burned, casting a soft, inviting glow against the darkness of the night. Figures cloaked in robes of deep indigo and silver circled the fire, their faces obscured, yet their presence immensely powerful.

Lara paused at the edge of the clearing, her breath visible in the crisp air. One of the figures turned to her, and with a gentle gesture, invited her to join them. As she stepped into the circle, she felt a surge of energy rise from the earth, through her feet, igniting a warmth that spiraled up her spine.

The eldest of the group, a woman with eyes as clear as the night sky, stepped forward. Her voice was soft yet carried a weight that commanded attention. "Welcome, Lara, seeker of the mysteries. You have come to us at the time of the celestial alignment when the veil is thinnest, and the ancient wisdom can be transferred. Tonight, you will receive the knowledge that you have been preparing for all your life."

Lara bowed her head in respect and gratitude. The Elder continued, "Before you join us, you must first release the burdens of your worldly concerns and purify your spirit. Come."

She led Lara to a small basin filled with water that shimmered under the moonlight. "This water is collected from the sacred spring of Avalon, where the veils between worlds are forever thin. Wash your hands and face, and let go of that which does not serve your highest purpose."

As Lara touched the water, images flashed before her eyes—visions of her past struggles, her triumphs, and the myriad paths she had walked. With each image that surfaced, she felt a weight lifting from her shoulders, her spirit growing lighter and more attuned to the energy of the circle.

Cleansed and refreshed, she joined the Elders around the fire once more. The eldest handed her a small, leather-bound book, its pages edged with gold. "This is the Book of Shadows, containing the wisdom of the mystics who have walked this path before you. With this, you will learn the ways of the mystic, how to harness the energies of the earth, the stars, and all that lies between."

Lara accepted the book with trembling hands, aware of the responsibility now entrusted to her. The Elder spoke again, "With this knowledge comes a responsibility. You must use what you learn to heal, to enlighten, and to guide those who are lost in darkness. Are you prepared to accept this duty?"

"I am," Lara replied, her voice steady and clear.

The circle closed around her, and the Elders began to chant in an ancient language that resonated with Lara's soul. She felt her consciousness expanding, her perception of the world deepening. The fire seemed to dance to the rhythm of the chant, and the stars above shone with an intensity she had never noticed before.

As the chanting continued, the Elders each placed a hand on her shoulder, transferring their energy, their blessings, and their wisdom. The experience was overwhelming, yet Lara felt an inner strength rising within her, a power that she knew would guide her through the trials and tribulations of her mystical journey.

The ceremony concluded with the Elders embracing Lara, now one of their own. "You are ready, Mystic of the New Dawn," the eldest declared. "Go forth with the blessings of the ancients, the energy of the earth, and the light of the stars guiding you."

As she walked back through the forest, Lara felt changed. The night seemed alive with whispers of ancient secrets and the promise of mystical adventures yet to come. She knew this was just the beginning of her true journey into the realms of the mystics, a journey of discovery, transformation, and enlightenment.

She opened the Book of Shadows, its pages aglow with the fire's light, and began to read. Each word, each phrase took her deeper into the mysteries of the universe, offering her insights and knowledge that had been hidden from the uninitiated. Lara realized that this was not just a book; it was a gateway to understanding the interconnectedness of all things, the fabric of the cosmos woven through the tapestry of time.

As dawn approached, the first light of the morning sun touched the horizon, casting golden hues across the sky. Lara felt a profound peace settle over her. She had found her place within the Circle of Elders, and with it, the path to fulfilling her destiny as a mystic.

The journey ahead would be filled with challenges, but Lara knew she possessed the tools and the wisdom to face them. With the Book of Shadows as her guide, and the blessings of the Elders, she was ready to embark on her sacred mission to bring light to the darkest corners of the world.

Chapter 15: The Phoenix Fire

Beneath the canopy of an ancient, whispering forest, where the trees bore witness to millennia, Mara walked with a sense of purpose she had never felt before. The ground was soft beneath her feet, a carpet of moss and fallen leaves that muted her steps. Her heart was a mix of trepidation and excitement as she approached the legendary Phoenix Fire, a mystical flame said to grant rebirth and profound transformation to those brave enough to embrace its power.

As she ventured deeper into the woods, the air grew warmer, the scent of burning wood and resin filling her senses. Finally, she came upon a clearing where a great fire blazed in a stone pit, its flames dancing wildly under the moonlit sky. Around the fire, figures cloaked in shadow murmured chants that seemed to rise and weave through the smoke, reaching for the stars.

Mara approached slowly, her gaze locked on the fire. The elders had spoken of this moment, the ritual of the Phoenix Fire, where one faced their deepest fears and emerged anew. It was not just a test of courage but a profound spiritual cleansing, a death of the old self to make way for the new.

Standing at the edge of the fire, she was met by the High Mystic, a woman whose eyes shone with the wisdom of ages. With a gentle nod, the High Mystic invited Mara to step forward.

"Mara, child of the cosmos," the High Mystic began, her voice strong and clear, "you stand before the Phoenix Fire, the heart of transformation. Here, you must let go of all that binds you to your past, all fears, regrets, and pains. Are you prepared to let the flames consume these burdens?"

Mara nodded, feeling the weight of her past heavy on her shoulders. She was ready to let go, to be reborn from the ashes of her former self.

"Then step into the circle, and speak your truths into the fire. Let it take away what no longer serves you," instructed the High Mystic.

With a deep breath, Mara stepped into the circle of flames. The heat enveloped her, not burning, but warm and intense, like a loving embrace. She closed her eyes, and images of her past flashed before her—the doubts, the fears, the moments of despair.

"I release my fears," she spoke into the flames, her voice trembling but resolute. "I let go of the pain of lost loves, the bitterness of failures, and the shadows of loneliness. I am no longer bound by these."

As her words turned to smoke and rose with the flames, Mara felt a lightness spreading through her. The fire's heat grew stronger, more insistent, as if urging her to shed even more of her old self.

"I relinquish my resentments," Mara continued, her voice growing stronger. "The anger I held against those who wronged me, the self-pity I wallowed in. These too, I release into the fire."

The flames crackled and roared, as if celebrating each declaration of release, each surrender of pain and sorrow. Mara felt the fire's energy coursing through her, not just cleansing but empowering her.

With each confession, the fire blazed brighter, its golden light reflecting in Mara's eyes, now open and clear. She stood in the center of the flames, her heart exposed, her soul bare. And in that vulnerability, she found a profound strength, a fierce joy that she had never known.

"I am reborn!" Mara exclaimed, her voice echoing through the clearing. The fire surged, and for a moment, it seemed a phoenix formed within the flames, its wings spread wide, its cry a piercing melody of renewal.

The High Mystic stepped forward, her hands raised in blessing. "Mara, you have embraced the Phoenix Fire and have been reborn. Rise now, not as who you were, but as who you are meant to be. Embrace your rebirth, for you are the Phoenix risen from its ashes."

As the fire slowly died down to glowing embers, Mara stepped out of the circle, her face radiant, her eyes alight with new purpose. She felt lighter, free of the chains of her past, her spirit imbued with a fiery strength.

The elders and other mystics came forward, encircling her with smiles and warm embraces. They sang songs of rebirth and danced under the moonlight, celebrating Mara's transformation.

In the days that followed, Mara noticed changes within herself. She moved with a new grace, spoke with newfound authority, and faced challenges with a calm certainty. The ritual of the Phoenix Fire had not just burned away her past burdens; it had ignited a spark within her, a flame that would guide her as she walked her path as a mystic.

Through the ritual of the Phoenix Fire, Mara had learned a profound truth: in every ending, there is a beginning, and in the ashes of what was, lies the potential for what will be. And with this knowledge, she moved forward, her heart ablaze with the light of her reborn soul, ready to meet her destiny.

Chapter 16: The Labyrinth Walk

As the morning mist hugged the contours of the forest floor, Alia stood at the entrance of the ancient labyrinth, its worn stones peeking out from a carpet of moss and leaves. The air was thick with the scent of earth and the faint trace of jasmine, a sacred fragrance said to favor the path of the seekers. Today, she was more than just a seeker; she was a pilgrim in the sacred journey of her soul, about to embark on the labyrinth walk that promised to offer clarity and direction to those who walked its path with a true heart.

The labyrinth was no ordinary maze. There were no dead ends, only a single convoluted path that led to the center and back out again, mirroring the journey of life with all its twists and turns, its retreats and advances. It was a tool for meditation and spiritual guidance, used by mystics and sages for centuries as a way to quiet the mind and find deeper truths.

Alia took a deep breath, closed her eyes for a moment, and stepped forward onto the path. The cool stone beneath her bare feet grounded her to the earth. With each step, she let go of the external noise, the chatter of her thoughts, and the weight of her doubts. The journey into the labyrinth was a metaphor for her journey inward, to the core of her being where her deepest truths lay hidden.

As she walked, Alia reflected on her journey thus far. She had encountered mystical experiences that had challenged her perception of reality and had brought her to this sacred place. Now, amidst the turning path, she sought answers to questions she had barely dared to ask aloud. Why was she chosen to walk this mystic path? What was she meant to find at the center of this labyrinth?

The path curved sharply, and she followed its bend with a practiced ease, her mind settling into a meditative rhythm. The deeper into the labyrinth she walked, the more her senses heightened. The rustle of the leaves seemed to whisper secrets, and the wind carried voices of the past, murmuring tales of those who had walked this path before her.

Halfway to the center, Alia paused. Here, the path looped back on itself, coming tantalizingly close to the center before veering away. It was a test of patience and commitment, reflecting the mystic's journey where insights often felt just out of reach, and understanding came not all at once, but in fleeting glimpses. She closed her eyes, took a deep breath, and focused on her heart's steady rhythm, letting it guide her forward.

As she approached the center of the labyrinth, her mind cleared, and a profound stillness enveloped her. The center opened up like a small clearing, encircled by stones that seemed to pulse with ancient energy. Stepping into the center, Alia felt as if she had stepped into the heart of the universe itself, where all was interconnected and every whisper of the wind held wisdom.

Here, in the sacred center, Alia sat down, crossing her legs and resting her hands on her knees. She closed her eyes and allowed herself to feel the energy of the place. It surged around her, through her, linking her to the labyrinth, the forest, and the vast, unseen cosmos.

In this moment of profound connection, Alia meditated on her purpose. The labyrinth had brought her to its heart, but it was her own heart that would provide the answers she sought. As she meditated, images danced behind her closed lids—visions of her past experiences, the challenges she had faced, and the lessons she had learned. Each vision was a thread in the tapestry of her life, and as she observed them, she began to see the pattern that they formed.

The meditation deepened, time seemed to stretch and bend, and a sense of peace settled over her. When at last she opened her eyes, the world seemed brighter, the colors more vivid, and the air fresher than before. She understood now that her journey was not just about seeking truth in the external world, but about recognizing the truths that lay within her.

With a newfound clarity, Alia rose from her seated position at the center of the labyrinth. As she walked the path back out, retracing her steps through the twists and turns, she felt each step affirming the insights she had gained. The labyrinth no longer felt like a puzzle to be solved, but like a reflection of her own journey, symbolizing the intricate and beautiful path of her life.

Exiting the labyrinth, she felt reborn in some essential way, as if she had shed an old skin and stepped out newer, truer to herself. She knew that the labyrinth would remain a part of her, a symbol of her journey and a reminder of the deep inner work she had undertaken. As the sun broke through the morning mist, casting light on the labyrinth stones, Alia turned and took one last look at the sacred path. She knew she would carry its lessons with her as she continued on her mystic journey, each step guided by the wisdom of the labyrinth. With a heart full of gratitude, she stepped away, her spirit light and ready for whatever path lay ahead.

Chapter 17: The Feast of Echoes

In the remote village where the mystic Amara had been born, there was an ancient tradition known only to a select few. Once a year, as the moon reached its fullest and brightest, a mystical feast was prepared, known as the Feast of Echoes. This was not just any feast; it was a divine communion where each morsel served was not merely food but a portal to the eater's past lives, echoing lessons and memories that were meant to guide and heal.

Amara, having been initiated into the mysteries of her lineage, was to host this year's feast for the first time. The preparations began at dawn. She gathered herbs from the sacred grove, each plant whispering secrets to her as she plucked leaves tenderly between her fingers. These herbs were ancient; some said they had been sown by the gods themselves, blessed with the power to unlock the deepest recesses of the soul.

As the sun dipped below the horizon, the villagers, cloaked in garments of deep blues and purples, began to arrive at Amara's small but welcoming cottage. Inside, the air was fragrant with the scents of roasting roots and simmering broths. Each dish was carefully laid out on a long wooden table, glowing under candles that flickered like tiny stars captured for this very night.

Amara welcomed her guests with a gentle nod, her eyes gleaming with the knowledge of the transformation that awaited them. As everyone settled, she stood at the head of the table, her voice soft yet carrying through the candle-lit room.

"Tonight, we partake in the Feast of Echoes, a meal that is a gateway to our pasts. Let each bite take you on a journey through the lives you have lived, the lessons you have learned, and the echoes of your eternal soul."

With a graceful wave of her hand, the feast began. The first course was a delicate soup made with the sacred herbs and infused with a broth that shimmered under the candlelight. As the villagers sipped the soup, their eyes closed, faces slack with the weight of centuries rolling back. Murmurs filled the room, some of joy, others of sorrow, as forgotten memories surfaced, as vivid as if they were reliving them in the moment.

Amara watched, her heart full of empathy for the journey her villagers undertook. The next course was served; a platter of roasted roots seasoned with spices that had been traded across deserts and oceans, reaching their village laden with the history of the world. Each root was carved in symbols that represented different epochs of time. Eating them was like walking through those eras, feeling the sand of ancient deserts underfoot, hearing the bustling markets of medieval ports, or sensing the chill of ice ages past.

As the feast continued, each course delved deeper into different aspects of the soul's journey. There was a salad of wild greens that tasted of victories, their crispness bursting with the exhilaration of battles won and challenges overcome. A stew of legumes and grains followed, each spoonful a comforting embrace, resonating with the warmth of love experienced and lost, of friendships that had spanned lifetimes.

The final dish was the most profound: a dessert of fruits drizzled with a syrup that sparkled like liquid starlight. Eating it was akin to experiencing the very birth and rebirth of the universe, the sweetness encapsulating the joy of creation, the tang of the fruits speaking to the inevitable decay and endings that made way for new beginnings.

As the meal concluded, Amara led her guests outside, where the full moon bathed them in its silvery glow. They formed a circle, hands joined, feeling the interconnectedness of their journeys, their lives woven together through the tapestry of time.

"Let us meditate on what we have remembered tonight," Amara instructed, her voice a soothing balm in the cool night air. "Close your eyes, breathe deep, and let the echoes of your souls guide you to the wisdom you need in this life."

The group fell silent, each person lost in reflection. The meditation was deep and profound, with each breath drawing up the sediment of lifetimes, filtering it through the soul's current needs and lessons. Insights sparked like fireflies in the dark, illuminating paths forward, healing old wounds, and empowering the villagers with the wisdom of ages.

When they finally opened their eyes, the moon was high overhead, casting its benevolent light over them. The air was charged with a palpable sense of renewal and clarity. Amara, feeling the weight and the warmth of her role as the mystic of the village, smiled softly.

"Carry these lessons forward," she said, her voice both a command and a benediction. "Let the echoes of your past enrich your present and guide your future. This is the gift of the Feast of Echoes, a reminder that we are all eternal, all connected, and forever guided by the wisdom of the lives we've lived."

The villagers departed slowly, their steps light, their hearts heavy with the magnitude of what they had experienced. Amara remained outside, looking up at the moon, a silent sentinel in her journey as a mystic, her soul resonating with the ancient echoes of her own past lives, ready to guide her as she embraced the path laid out before her.

Chapter 18: The Mirror of Galadriel

In the heart of the ancient forest, shrouded in a mist that whispered secrets of old, lay the Mirror of Galadriel. It was said that this mystical artifact could show the beholder not just their reflection but their true essence, their past wounds, and occasionally, glimpses of their potential futures. For our protagonist, Lysandra, finding the Mirror was not just a goal; it was a calling that resonated with the very core of her spirit.

As she trudged through the undergrowth, the trees seemed to lean closer, their branches intertwining to form archaic symbols. The forest felt alive, pulsating with an energy that Lysandra had learned to recognize and respect throughout her mystical journey. The leaves rustled with the energy of whispered wisdom, guiding her steps.

Finally, she stood before the clearing where the Mirror was said to reside. The air here was still, as if the forest itself held its breath in anticipation. In the center, the Mirror stood, its surface shimmering with an ethereal light that seemed to pulse gently, like the beating heart of the forest.

Lysandra approached with reverence, her heart pounding in her chest. She had faced many trials, each a preparation for this moment. The mystics had warned her that the Mirror would reveal truths that might shake the very foundations of her soul, but they had also promised it would grant her the wisdom to embrace her destiny.

Taking a deep breath, Lysandra stood before the Mirror. Instead of her physical reflection, she saw a mosaic of images, each a snapshot of her life. There she was as a child, hiding behind her mother during a storm, her young eyes wide with fear. Then as a teenager, standing atop a hill, her arms wide open as if she could embrace the whole world.

With each image, emotions surged through her—fear, joy, pain, love—each a thread in the tapestry of her being. The Mirror was not showing her what she looked like; it was showing her who she was.

But the journey through her past was just the beginning. The images shifted, becoming darker, more intense. She saw herself at her lowest moments, times when despair had gripped her heart. Yet, within these scenes, there was a light, a gentle but firm presence that had guided her through. It was the presence of the goddess, always there, her hand upon Lysandra's shoulder, even when she felt most alone.

The realization brought tears to her eyes. All this time, she had not been alone. Her journey, her pain, her joys, and her triumphs were all shared with the divine.

As the scenes faded, the Mirror's surface rippled, and a new vision began to form. It was Lysandra, but stronger, more serene, standing atop a mountain with her hands raised to the sky. Energy radiated from her, a bright, shining light that seemed to pierce the heavens. This was not a potential future; it was a promise of what she could become if she accepted her inner power and wisdom.

The vision slowly dissolved, and Lysandra was left staring at her own reflection. But now, she saw herself differently. The fear and uncertainty that had once clouded her eyes were gone, replaced by a calm certainty and profound strength.

She reached out, touching the cool surface of the Mirror, half-expecting it to ripple under her fingertips.

But it was solid, as real as the path she had walked to get here.

Stepping back, Lysandra took a moment to reflect on everything the Mirror had shown her. She understood now that her journey was not just about seeking mystical knowledge; it was about discovering herself, about healing the wounds of her past and embracing her true potential.

With a deep, cleansing breath, she prepared for the final part of this ritual: the meditation of acceptance. Sitting cross-legged in front of the Mirror, Lysandra closed her eyes and began to meditate, focusing on her breathing. In her mind's eye, she revisited each vision the Mirror had shown her, not as a passive observer, but as an active participant.

She felt the fear of the child and soothed it with the comfort of her adult wisdom. She revisited the joy of the teenager and amplified it with her gratitude. She embraced the pain of her darkest moments and infused them with the light of understanding and the presence of the goddess.

As the meditation deepened, Lysandra felt a profound shift within her. It was as if each piece of her being, once scattered and disconnected, was coming together, forming a whole that was greater than the sum of its parts. She was not just becoming the woman in the vision; she was becoming the woman she was meant to be—whole, healed, and powerful.

When she opened her eyes, the world seemed different—brighter, more vibrant. She stood up, facing the Mirror once again. This time, she saw just her reflection, but it was enough. Because in her eyes, there was now a spark, a visible manifestation of her mystical journey and her newfound wisdom.

With a respectful nod to the Mirror, Lysandra turned and walked back through the forest. The path home was the same, yet she was not the same person who had walked it before. She was a mystic, a seeker of truths, and a vessel of divine power. And she was ready to fulfill her destiny, whatever it might be, with grace, courage, and the wisdom of the goddess guiding her every step.

Chapter 19: The Oracle's Prophecy

The air was thick with the scent of juniper and myrrh as Selene entered the dimly lit chamber of the Oracle. The walls, etched with ancient runes and symbols, seemed to pulse with a life of their own under the flicker of torchlight. Selene's heart beat in sync with the primal drumming that filled the space, a sound that seemed to come from the very earth beneath her feet.

As she approached the center of the room, her eyes settled on the Oracle, an ageless figure shrouded in layers of silver and blue robes, her face obscured by the shadow of her hood. The Oracle's presence was both comforting and unnerving, embodying the duality of known and unknown, seen and unseen.

"Selene, seeker of the mystic truths," the Oracle's voice echoed in the cavernous room, "you have journeyed far and faced the shadows within and without. You stand at the precipice of your transformation. Are you prepared to hear what the future holds?"

Selene nodded, her resolve firm. "I am ready, Oracle. I seek guidance for the path that lies ahead."

The Oracle extended her hands over a small, black pool of water that shimmered against the stone floor, gesturing for Selene to come closer. As Selene stepped forward, she peered into the pool, and it seemed as though the water began to glow from within, casting a soft light that illuminated their faces.

"Look into the waters of fate," the Oracle instructed, her voice a whisper that seemed to reverberate deep within Selene's soul.

Selene obeyed, her gaze fixed on the liquid mirror. The water stilled under her intent look, and images began to swirl within its depths. Scenes of her past experiences flashed by—the sacred grove, the ritual of silence, the chalice of visions—all moments that had led her to this very point. But then the visions shifted, revealing scenes she had not yet lived. She saw herself standing atop a high cliff overlooking a sea that stretched into infinity. Stars shone brightly above her, and she was not alone. Figures cloaked in radiant garments of many colors surrounded her, their faces serene and wise.

"This is your future," the Oracle's voice pulled her back to the present. "You are to lead, Selene. The path of the mystic is solitary, but it also converges with the paths of others. You will find and guide the seekers of light, just as you have been guided."

Tears formed in Selene's eyes as the weight of this revelation settled upon her. She felt both honored and overwhelmed. "How will I know the way? How will I recognize the seekers?"

"The same way you have found your path—through the signs and symbols that resonate with your soul," the Oracle replied. "Trust in the visions you receive. Trust in the energies you feel. Your intuition has been honed by your trials and will be your most reliable guide."

Selene took a deep breath, absorbing the truth of these words. The visions in the pool faded, and she looked up into the face of the Oracle, seeking any further wisdom the mystic might offer.

"You must also prepare for challenges, Selene. Not all are ready for the light you will bring. Some dwell comfortably in shadow and will resist the change you embody. Remember, the strength you have built in facing your own shadows will serve you in facing those of the world."

"I understand," Selene responded, a new determination steeling her features. "And I am ready."

The Oracle smiled, a rare and enigmatic curl of the lips. "Then go forth, Selene. Your journey continues beyond the confines of this sacred space. You leave here not just as a seeker but as a bearer of light. The prophecy is set, but remember, every step you take is yours to choose. The future is not fixed; it is influenced by your actions and decisions."

With a final bow to the Oracle, Selene turned and walked towards the entrance of the chamber. The drumming had ceased, and in the silence, she felt a profound peace settle over her. The chamber door opened before her, leading back into the world that awaited her newfound purpose.

Outside, the night was clear, and the moon, her namesake, hung low and full in the sky. Selene paused to let the cool air fill her lungs, her mind replaying the Oracle's words. A sense of purpose ignited within her, warming her against the night's chill.

The path forward was not clear, nor was it certain, but Selene knew she was not alone. The visions in the water had shown her future companions, and her heart told her that she would meet them soon. With a final look at the moon, she set off into the night, ready to embrace her destiny, whatever it might hold.

Chapter 20: The Ascension

As Aria stood at the edge of the cliff, overlooking the vast, shimmering ocean under the blanket of stars, she felt the culmination of her journey pulsing through her veins. The cool night breeze whispered ancient secrets, carrying the scent of salt and freedom. This was the moment she had been preparing for—the final step in her transformation into a mystic of the highest order.

Her journey had been arduous and enlightening, filled with trials that tested her resolve and moments of profound revelation that uplifted her spirit. From the day she had first experienced the thinning veil between the worlds to her encounters with divine entities and her mastery of mystical arts, each step had brought her closer to this pinnacle.

Now, as she prepared for her ascension, Aria reflected on the key teachings she had absorbed from the mystic elders. The wisdom of the sacred grove, the healing powers of the mystic waters, the challenging shadow dances, and the balancing of divine energies—all these experiences had woven a rich tapestry of knowledge and skill within her.

She began her final ritual by setting up a small altar at the cliff's edge. Upon it, she placed symbols of her journey: a feather representing air and mental clarity, a small vial of seawater for emotional depth and healing, a stone for grounding and physical strength, and a flame within a lantern to symbolize the fire of her spirit. As she arranged these elements, she chanted a mantra of gratitude and readiness, her voice steady and clear.

Aria then sat cross-legged in front of the altar, closing her eyes to enter a state of deep meditation. She visualized herself as a tree, her roots extending deep into the earth, her branches reaching up to the sky. This imagery anchored her in the physical world while allowing her spirit to soar into the celestial realms.

In her meditative state, Aria traveled through a luminous portal that appeared in her mind's eye. This portal was no longer a mere visualization; it was as real as the wind on her skin. As she passed through it, she found herself in an ethereal realm filled with vibrant colors and transcendent music.

Here, in this otherworldly dimension, Aria encountered beings of pure energy—ascended mystics who had walked the path before her. They greeted her with warmth and recognition, for they had been guiding her since the beginning of her journey, though she had not always been aware of their presence.

One of the ascended mystics, a radiant figure enveloped in soft golden light, approached her. "Aria, you have reached the threshold of true mastery," the figure spoke, her voice echoing like a melody. "Your journey through the human realm has prepared you for this moment—the ascension into the mystic's true form."

Aria listened intently, absorbing every word. She was told about the responsibilities of an ascended mystic—how she would need to guide others on their paths, help maintain the balance between the physical and spiritual worlds, and continue her own spiritual growth in new and challenging ways.

As the explanation unfolded, Aria felt an overwhelming sense of purpose and joy. She realized that her personal transformation was part of a much larger tapestry of cosmic evolution. Each mystic's ascension added a thread of light to the fabric of the universe.

The ceremony of ascension was simple yet profound. The gathered mystics formed a circle around her, chanting in an ancient tongue as they raised their hands towards her. Aria felt a surge of energy coursing through her, lifting her from the ground. Her physical form began to dissolve into light, her essence merging with the divine energy of the mystics.

When the ceremony concluded, Aria found herself back at the cliff, still in her physical form, but irrevocably changed. She opened her eyes, feeling a new power and clarity. Her senses were heightened, her understanding of the mystical arts deepened, and her connection to the divine was unbreakable.

She stood up, her heart full of gratitude and her mind clear. As the first light of dawn touched the horizon, painting the sky with hues of orange and pink, Aria knew that her journey as a human mystic had ended, but her role in the greater cosmic dance was just beginning.

She took a deep breath, feeling the energy of the earth, the air, the water, and the fire within her. With a calm smile and a determined heart, she turned away from the cliff, ready to embark on her new path as an ascended mystic, a guide and protector of the spiritual and physical realms.

Aria's story was a testament to the power of faith, the richness of learning, and the beauty of spiritual evolution. Her ascension was not an end, but a glorious new beginning.

Printed in Great Britain
by Amazon

46789584R00056